GW00567320

THE ILLUSTRATED MOTORCYCLE LEGENDS

Kawasaki

ROY BACON

SUNBURST BOOKS

Previous page: The GPZ500S of 1987.

Acknowledgements

The author and publishers wish to acknowledge thelr debt to all who loaned material and photographs for this book. Most came from the Kawasaki Information Service which has been run for many years by Peter Richardson who was able to fill the gaps in the author's own files. Other pictures which helped to complete the story came from *Motor Cycle News* courtesy of editor Rob Munro-Hall and EMAP whose archives hold the old *Motor Cycle Weekly* files. Thanks to all who helped.

Published 1994 by Sunburst Books, Deacon House,
65 Old Church Street, London SW3 5BS exclusively
for Coles in Canada and Angus and Robertson in Australia.

ISBN 1 85778 038 8

Designed by Anthony Cohen

Printed and bound in China

Contents

ORIGINS

Kawasaki – largest and smallest of the Japanese motorcycle firms, a firm 'to let the good times. roll', the Green Meanies, and 'who can catch a Kawasaki'. Different from the others but no less successful, often the market leader and known as 'King of the road'. In time, the name simply meant - 'Performance'.

Kawasaki Heavy Industries originated. in 1878 when Shozo Kawasaki founded a shipyard at Tsukiji, Tokyo, from which came an industrial giant. Ships, trains, civil engineering, steel works, aircraft, all became part of the massive conglomerate which was one of the original *zaibatsu*, the economic cartels which drove Japan from feudal to industrial so quickly.

There was a tentative involvement with motorcycles and their engines in the early-1950s, but it was 1962 before the first Kawasaki machine, a modest 125, appeared, and then essentially as a means of promoting the company name. Although well known and respected in its fields, the firm was little known to the public at large, so the motorcycles came as a means to correct this

Earlier, the firm had become involved with Meguro, a pre-war Japanese motorcycle firm who later became best known for a twin modelled on a BSA. They established the Meihatsu name for a range using Kawasaki engines, but these had limited success, although this activity gave them a grounding in the business.

This is Kawasaki Heavy Industries - and it all began with ships.

And there were trains.

and planes.

and chemical plant construction.

- and finally motorcycles, this being a1992 ZZ-R1100, one of their hyper-sports series.

First machine to carry the Kawasaki name was this 125cc B8 of 1962.

The 1964 248cc SG was based on an earlier Meguro single, rugged and reliable.

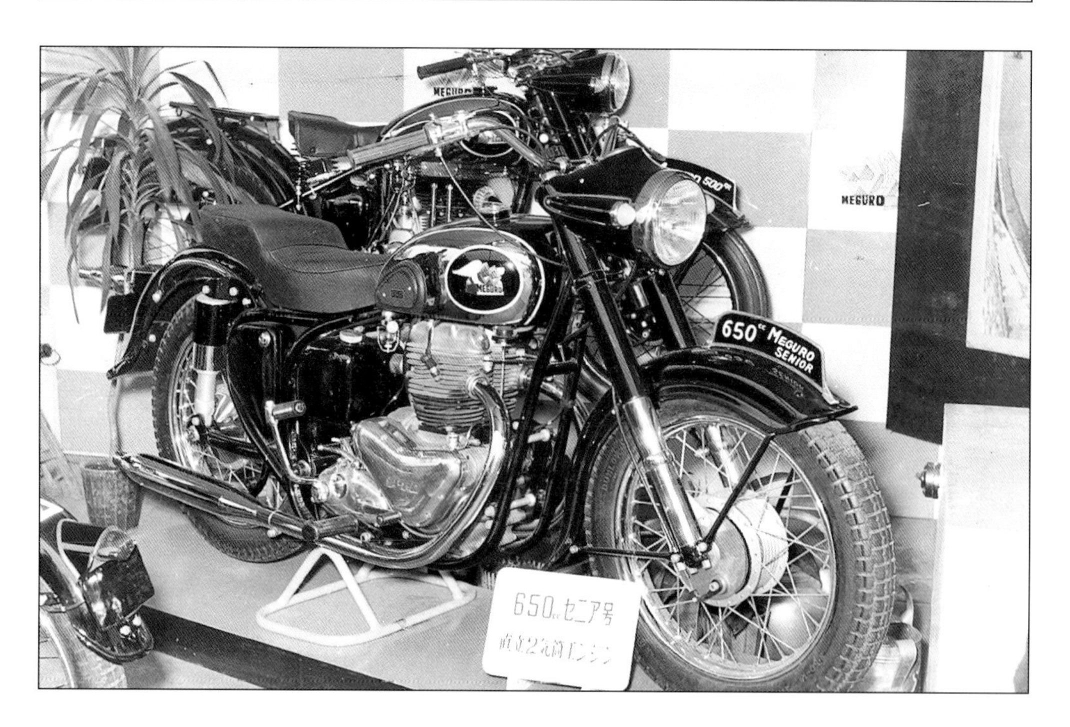

Postwar Meguro twin which had a BSA line and later became a Kawasaki model, this the 650cc version.

This 1961 B7 Meihatsu was the first machine completely built by Kawasaki who established the name in 1953.

FIRST STEPS

When Kawasaki launched their first model the other major Japanese firms were already heavily engaged in European Grand Prix racing to promote their products. Only interested in home market sales and publicity, Kawasaki turned to Japanese motocross races using their one model. Tuned, and with the tank painted, it won, and the 'Red Tank Kawasaki' was a slogan to advertise. It was a promotional method they would use again.

Kawasaki began to export to the USA in the mid-1960s, and to Europe a little later. Much of their extensive range was kept at home, mainly small two-stroke singles built in a bewildering array of types for road or trail use, one even offered as a farm bike complete with spade! All were basic, worthy and well made. Many stayed in the lists for year after year, often only altering the colour and graphics, sometimes with an update to the mechanics. Thus, today's KH125 can trace its lineage right back to the B8 model of 1962.

However, Kawasaki wanted their name to be promoted and chose the performance route as the means to do this. Their extensive range of singles allowed them to serve their home market and build a manufacturing base, but could never offer the glamour the export fields demanded. They did dip an early toe in competition waters, Meguro having run at the 1957 Asama meeting in Japan, but it was not until 1965 that Kawasaki contested the Japanese GP using a 125cc twin, while the next two years saw them at the same race running both a twin and a four in the 125cc class. It was 1969 before these grand prix efforts paid off when Dave Simmonds took the 125cc world title with eight wins and two seconds, including a TT win.

By then, Kawasaki were firmly set on the performance route, although their first attempt proved abortive. They took the old Meguro four-stroke twin which had the look of a BSA Golden Flash twin and stretched it out to 624cc. Internally the engine differed in many ways from the BSA, although the concept followed true, and the model sold well in Japan. In the USA it failed. The word soon went round that the real British twins were better and attempts to jazz up the old Meguro design had no effect at all. Bright colours, sports fittings, a model having waist-level exhausts, all were tried and none captured the American imagination - maybe because the style was too much BSA. Customers for that bought the original, others sought something different and went elsewhere.

The moto-cross B8M was based on the works 'Red Tank Kawasaki' and successful.

Farm bike, complete with spade, the 100cc 'Agi Bike' of 1974.

Early road single, the 1968 125cc B1TL was based on the B8 and led to the KC125 built up to 1980.

This 1985 KH125 demonstrates both technical advance and stability from the machlnes of three decades earlier.

At the bottom of the range were these small singles, of 50 or 52cc, built from 1965-69.

Trail 175 of 1967, typical of the type and based on a similar road model.

The 125cc racing twin of 1965, later taken to the 1969 world title by Dave Simmonds.

The 1967 works 125cc four only ever run in Japan.

Based on the Meguro, this W1 had a 624cc engine, looked like a BSA, sold well in Japan, but not in the USA.

More sporting version was this W2SS, but it failed to catch on in America, maybe due to that BSA line, obsolete by 1968.

HOT TWINS

Kawasaki decided to try another tack, concentrating on acceleration for the traffic light grand prix. This mattered to many buyers, more so than high-speed cruising, economy, pure top speed although that could never be discounted, or the subtleties of handling and suspension.

This time they went for light weight and two-stroke power, having learnt about that from the grand prix racing. The outcome was the 250cc Samurai, a machine having a twin-cylinder two-stroke engine with disc inlet valves, a five-speed gearbox and plenty of power. It was launched in May 1966 and quickly made its presence felt on the streets, outdragging far larger machines to promote the Kawasaki name and image.

At the end of the year it was joined by a road-racing machine, the A1R, which ran well, but of more importance was the larger 338cc model which appeared early in 1967. Named Avenger, it offered more cubes to the Americans and was a flyer on the street. At the same time a street scrambler version of the Samurai was introduced as the A1SS, this having both exhaust systems high on the left and fitted with perforated heat shields for rider protection. Late in 1967 a similar Avenger was listed as the A7SS and was jolned by a racing model, the A7R, for 1968.

Kawasaki found that they had most of the answer as the twins would streak away from the big four-strokes when the lights went green. By the time the larger machines had got into their stride and were running faster, the next set of lights had come up red and the contest was all set to start again. Only when there was a long stretch of road could the 650s catch up and pull away, using their greater power and top-end speed. They may have used less fuel but at that time few cared, acceleration from the lights was what counted.

The two-stroke twins, along with the old ohv twin, ran on to the start of the 1970s, but Kawasaki were already pushing ahead down two totally different avenues, one of raw power, the other of sophistication and destined to run and run. Both were to totally outperform existing machines and to introduce new standards on the road.

The 1967 250cc Samurai twln which began the Kawasakl performance legend, outperforming many larger models on the street.

Racing version of the Samurai, the A1R which was quick.

Avenger 338cc twin which followed the 250 early in 1967.

Above:The A1SS Street Scrambler Samurai had stylish exhaust systems to distinguish it.

The racing A7R, here finished in Kawasaki lime green, was based on the road twin.

Kawasaki continued to offer competition models such as this 250cc moto-cross F21M single listed for 1968-70.

THIRSTY TRIPLES

The first new machine came in 1968 with the advent of the 499cc Mach III, a model powered by a three-cylinder, two-stroke engine and offering performance, excitement, wild acceleration and a staggering top speed for the time. The triple had its air-cooled engine set across the frame, this fed by a bank of carburettors, ignited by an early form of electronic ignition, and exhausted into three systems, two fitted on the right.

An output of 60bhp, an engine carried a little too far back in the frame, low weight and a power curve that took off at 6000rpm, all contributed to the model's character and legend. It was the immediate master of the traffic light grand prix, and its outrageous performance coupled with indifferent handling, made it a machine to love or hate, but in either case to respect or it would bite. Safety, fuel economy, ecology or being plain sensible had nothing to do with it - hence its success.

Listed as the H1, the first triple was soon joined by others. First came a racing version, destined to win at grand prix and TT level, then 250, 350 and 750cc versions for 1971, the last to set new standards for road machines. It was also the basis of a racing version for the works which, finished in a lime green matched by the riders' leathers, became known as Green Meanies. Fast, brutal and hard to handle at first, but successful.

In time the triples were overshadowed and the excitement of the early machines gradually faded as they were partly civilised and lost the raw edges that made them what they really were. The 350 became a 400 but the 750 went in 1975, the 500 a year later, to leave just the 250 and 400 to run on to 1980, still offering an exciting, thirsty ride. Then they were gone.

The Mach III offered staggering performance from its 499cc, three-cylinder engine, an immediate legend.

Left: A complete contrast, the 1969 MB1 Coyote which used a 133cc side-valve engine to create a run-about.

Below: The air-cooled racing triple H2R without fairing, a machine which won some good races.

Smallest triple was this 250cc S1 Mach I.

Next in size came the 350cc S2 Mach II for a year or two.

Largest was the 750cc H2 Mach IV, a rocket ship for its time.

Green Meanie, the works, watercooled racing 750 seen at Brands Hatch in 1979, Barry Ditchburn up.

The 350 triple grew into the 400cc S3, later the KH400, offering an exciting ride and hefty thirst for fuel.

KING OF THE ROAD

Meanwhile, back in 1967, Kawasaki were working on something else in total contrast, a sophisticated four-cylinder four-stroke. The aim was to offer this at the start of the 1970s, the complete opposite to the triple they were about to unleash, but equalling it in acceleration and top speed. Then came the 1968 Tokyo Show and the Honda CB750. Oriental faces wore a mask and the project stopped.

However, Kawasaki were able to dissect the Honda and watch its success. The outcome was a programme revival to upstage their rivals by offering more engine capacity and not one but two overhead camshafts. The result was launched at Cologne in September 1972 as the Z1, a 903cc four having twin camshafts, five gears, disc front brake, electric start and all the features expected of such a machine.

Large and heavy it might have been, but the Z1 turned in a consistent 130mph and a low 12 second quarter time. It soon carried the name of 'King of the road', being quickly joined by a 750cc version for the Japanese market. It took world long-distance records and in 1974 and 1975 Kawasaki went endurance racing with the Z1, achieving great success in the major events.

The King of the Road Z1 on its launch in Britain, 903cc, four cylinders and twin camshafts added up to an impressive package.

The 1975 Z1B had this colour and finlsh to set it off.

Cutaway engine of the Z1, a tough unit able to run fast and hard for great distances.

Far right: Clocks and warning lights of the first Z1, 130 mph was there for the asklng.

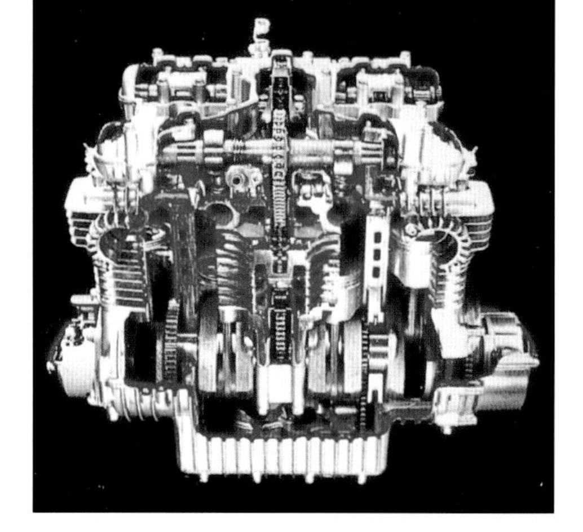

Below: Kawasaki took the Z1 endurance racing wlth great success, Godier and Genoud winning many events in 1974-75.

EXPANSION

Kawasaki now spelt performance with civilisation as the hot triples faded from the scene and the firm quickly built up a four-stroke range. The first to join the Z1 was the Z400 in 1974, a twin-cylinder model having a single overhead camshaft, five speeds, disc front brake and electric start. Inside the engine there were dynamic balancers to cut the vibrations felt by the rider. A year later it was joined by a drum-braked version which also lacked the electric leg. These models introduced the practice of incorporating the nominal engine capacity in the model code which continues with rare exceptions to this day.

The hoardes of small two-strokes kept going — the bread and butter machines essential for the factory and a broad product base. Often technically clever and innovative, built in numerous forms, revised each year but staying basically the same for many years. Alongside the road models there were trail, trial, enduro, agricultural and motocross models, all to progress through the years as development drove them forward.

For 1976 a larger twin, the Z750, was added, this having a twin-cam engine, while the Z1 changed its name to the Z900 and added a second front disc. It was joined by the Z900LTD, a custom model having cast-alloy wheels, disc rear brake, four-into-two exhaust, and the stepped seat of the style. Once again the firm was moving into a new area, one where they were to stay with success and be joined by others.

The large fours went up in capacity for 1977, becoming the Z1000 and Z1000LTD, and were joined by the Z650, another four in the same mould, offered with either wire-spoke or cast-alloy wheels, the latter having dual front and single rear disc brakes A further new model was the Z200, a single having a single camshaft, electric start and a mechanical dlsc brake. It was a useful commuter tool and offered a change from the small two-strokes.

Next four-stroke model was the Z400, a twin having a single camshaft.

Simple and basic 100cc GA5, one of the many small models.

This KV100 had a dual-range transmission, the five-speed gearbox being coupled to a two-speed range to give ten ratios in all.

Moto-cross machines came in three sizes, the smallest this KX125.

For the next class in moto-cross there was the KX250

Above: Top of the moto-cross range was this KX400, fast and listed for experts only.

An off-road, trail model was this KS125 which featured a six-speed gearbox.

Another off-road version was the KD125 which was without lights and had more suitable tyres.

For trials use there was the KT250 with plenty of ground clearance.

Fun time off-road was the province of this mini KV75, one of a series.

More serious but still a fun bike was this KM90 mini.

Later bored out to become the KM100, still off-road and dual purpose, this a 1980 version.

While the KD100 was the same minus the lights but plus better tyres.

The KE100 was aimed more at the street although remainlng a dual purpose model.

For pure road use there was the KH100, a good commuter model.

Larger in capacity but still set up for the more serious off-road rider was this KD175.

The KE175 was the street model with some off-road abilities.

Below: Smaller in size but able to hold its own was the KE125.

The Z750 twin was added to the range for 1976.

The Z1 was renamed Z900 for 1976, being improved in detail only.

First LTD model was the 900 of 1976, enlarged to this Z1000LTD the next year.

Z1000 of 1977, larger and improved from the first Z1.

Some of the detail features of the Z1000.

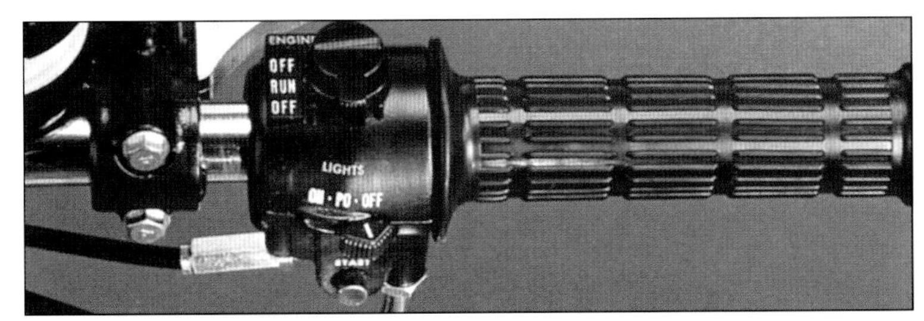

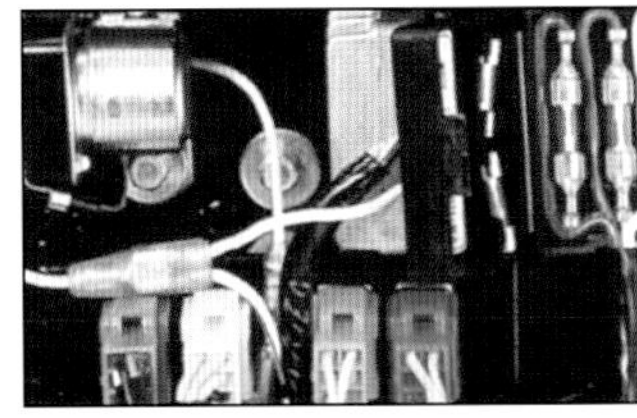

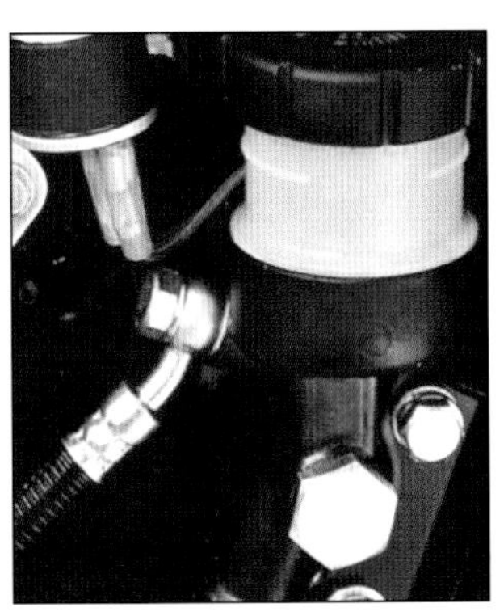

The Z650 came for 1977, much in the Kawasaki-four mould.

Fitted with cast-alloy wheels, the model became the Z650C.

A smaller single was this Z200 with one camshaft.

Another version of the two-stroke single came as the KH100EL.

Larger and having a disc front brake was the KH125A.

TRAIL, CUSTOM & RACING

The Z200 was joined by an enlarged trail model, the KL250, for 1978, this having suitable changes for off-road work. There was also another version of the Z650, this having crossover exhaust pipes among its features, and the ZIR. The latter was based on the Z1000 but came with the cast wheels, a cockpit fairing, revised style and an engine finished in black, offset by the general colour of metallic stardust silver.

That same year saw Kawasaki enhance their competition record at grand prix level for Kork Ballington won both 250 and 350cc world titles. The machines he used were nearly identical, having tandem twin two-stroke engines whose cylinders fired together to give a flat exhaust note compared to the opposition. It sounded slow but the Kawasakis had the legs of the field.

So much so that Ballington repeated his success in 1979 but had to miss several races in 1980 due to illness. However, Anton Mang took up the gauntlet for Kawasaki to take the 250 title, in which Ballington was still second, but lost the 350 one by a small margin. That year also saw Ballington out on a 500cc four, its engine in a square-four layout so essentially based on two tandem twins. The machine used a light alloy monocoque frame and rising-rate suspension developed on the racing twins and to go into stock production machines. It was never to win a grand prix but Mang won both the 250 and 350 titles in 1981 and took the 350 one in 1982, the last year it was run. With eight titles in five years, Kawasaki packed up and went home.

Earlier, in 1978, they had been involved with Don Vesco when he moved the motorcycle world speed record on to 318.598mph. For this he ran a full streamliner fitted with two turbo-charged fours, one behind the other. Two toothed belts, one on each side, joined the engines which packed tightly into the shell along with all the pipes, wires and hoses needed to keep them on song.

First of the four-stroke trail models was the KL250 whose engine was based on the road Z200.

The Z650D had its exhaust pipes crossed for an Amerircan style.

The moto-cross models continued to improve, this being the 1978 KX125.

By adding a cockpit fairing and other styling changes, the Z1-R was created.

Top view of the Z1-R

Above: The KR tandem-twin Kawasaki on which Kork Ballington and Anton Mang won eight world titles, this the 250.

Left: Kork Ballington riding the KR500 four-cylinder racer, competitive but destined never to win a grand prix.

Right: Belt drive tried on the 250 racing machine, later to find itself on the road machines.

MORE & MORE MODELS

Among the road models most of the old continued into 1979, joined by more new four-strokes. Smallest of these was the Z250 Scorpion, a twin much as the Z400, and the KLX250, much as the off-road single but aimed more at the enduro rider so without lights at first. Two more twins appeared as the Z400G, a custom model with cast wheels, and the Z400LTD, a US custom with pull-back bars, stepped seat, fat rear tyre and shorty mufflers.

In Europe the interest was more on the Z500, a new four in the Z1 tradition, while the various Z650s ran on in stock and custom forms. A Z750 four was listed only for South Africa that year, while the Z1000 became two models, the MkII much as before and the ST which had shaft drive.

Below: Small road twin, the Z250A as in 1980.

Enduro KLX250 appeared for 1979, using the single engine and without lights at first.

Junior KX80 moto-cross machine offered for several years, this the 1979 model.

Some custom features turned the stock twin into the Z400G; with pull-back bars and stepped seat it became the US Z400LTD.

Mid-range four that found favour with rlders was this Z500.

Above: One of two big fours for 1979 was this Z1000Mk.II which had chain final drive.

Right: The other four was the Z1000ST with shaft drive, both could reach 135mph and were fine, comfortable machines.

SIX, GPZ & TURBO

Finally, Kawasaki unveiled their answer to Honda's CBX. Like that model, the Z1300 had six cylinders, but it was larger, water-cooled and a monster of a machine. For all that, it stayed around for a decade with minimal alteration. It was also offered fitted with a fairing, panniers, top box and special touring seat in 1980, but this version was dropped after a year or so.

Newcomers for 1980 included a cheaper version of the Scorpion along with stock and custom versions of a Z250 single, all of which resulted in some customer confusion with model types. The Z250 now existed in A, B, C, D and G forms, C the single and G the custom, while D was another custom single having wire wheels. And there was still the KH250 triple in the lists as well as the off-road models.

A little up the scale the Z400 twins were joined by the Z400J, a four-cylinder road model, plus the Z440, a twin offered in road and custom styles, and the Z550, yet another four in both forms. Then there were the Z750 fours, now generally available to all in road or custom form and the custom Z750LTD twin joined the list. At the top end of the scale came another Z1000, this time having electronic fuel injection, a production motorcycle first. It was an impressive range for a firm that had only began to build modern four-strokes in 1972.

The expansion continued into 1981, starting right at the bottom with 50 and 80cc models, both offered in road or trail forms, the latter styled to match competition trends, the former coming with cast wheels and a cockpit fairing. There were other small models but the real Kawasaki news was of the GPZ, a new sports line. This set

The Kawasaki monster, the massive six-cylinder Z1300, watercooled, heavy and able to cruise all day, every day.

Opposite end of the scale saw this neat KC100 appear to offer transport at minimal cost.

Above: Sectioned Z1300 mechanics; engine, gearbox, shaft drive and rear wheel.

new standards and began with two models, the GPZ550 and the GPZ1100, both fours in the firm's usual style, the larger a step up in capacity offered also as the Z1100, a tourer with shaft drive. There was also the Z1000LTD in the custom mould and an update for the sports Z1000.

The GPZ took the firm a step forward so there was no surprise when a GPZ750 appeared for 1982 but alongside it was the GT750, a shaft-drive tourer destined to become a despatch rider favourite. A new venture was the 750 Turbo, a route all the major firms tried but never to be a success with customers. At the other end the AR125 was introduced, a water-cooled model destined for a lengthy run in the lists. Styled with a cockpit fairing, it was built to suit the UK learner laws, but also listed in unrestricted form when it was a flyer. A second version of the Z440LTD was added, this having belt final drive, an innovative feature which was to appear on other models.

Both the sports and touring ranges were expanded for 1983 when the GPZ305, a twin styled to match the series, and the shaft drive GT550, were added. As with its larger companion, the new GT would still be listed a decade later. The year also brought the Z1000R, based on the existing four but fitted with a cockpit fairing and two level seat, this being joined by the larger Z1100R in the same style for 1984.

The Scorpion Z250 went on to use belt flnal drive and the Uni-Trak rear suspension developed in competition, thls belng a 1984 model.

A single-cylinder Z250 was listed along with the twin, based on the earlier Z200.

Custom version of the single was this Z250LTD, this one from 1982.

The trail KE175 in its 1980 form, continuing the series which ran for so long.

Revised as the Z400J for 1980, this four had the twin camshafts and a six-speed gearbox.

The middle-range twin was enlarged to create the Z440 for 1980, this being the 1982 model.

Along with the new twin there came a custom version, the Z440LTD, this the 1981 model.

With the addItion of the 400-four, the 500 was stretched out to become this Z550.

Further up the scale came this Z750 four, on general release in 1980, light and fast.

As was becoming their habit, Kawasaki offered the new model in a custom form as well as stock, this being the Z550LTD.

Above: A custom version of the four was also offered as the Z750LTD, having the usual stepped seat, hlgh bars and 16-inch rear wheel.

Right: An alternative for the custom rider was this Z750LTD Twin, based on the model first seen back in 1976.

Fuel injection appeared on this Z1000H model of 1980, another step forward on the technical road.

New for 1981 was the road AR series fitted with cockpit fairing and offered in 50 and 80cc forms, this the larger model.

Matching the AR models were the AE in trail form, also offered as 50 and 80cc machines, this the smaller.

Variations of the small machines included this 1982 KE100, about to hand over to a new series after many years of service.

The new generation of the KE100, also a 1982 model, but with changes to ready it for the years to come.

On the road the KH100EX had cast-alloy wheels and a good in-town performance.

For slightly more power, there was the KH125, one of several variations.

Enduro KDX250 from 1981, offering moto-cross power and suspension with lights.

For the clubman there was the less powerful, but easier to ride, Enduro KLX250 having a four-stroke engine.

Pure moto-cross KX250 offered for out and out racing.

The new sports range was heralded by the GPZ550 four, the line of fairing, tank and seat to be common to the series.

Top end of the new 1981 series was this GPZ1100, a very quick motorcycle.

Touring riders were catered for by this Z1100 four which included shaft final drive in its specification.

Continuing the custom line was this 1982 version of the Z1000LTD.

Next in the sports line was this GPZ750 which continued the theme.

Having shaft drive and a good engine, this GT750 of 1982 soon became a despatch rider favourite.

Kawasaki went down the turbo route with this ZX750 but it was not to be popular.

Copying the sports style for beginners, this AR125 had street cred.

For 1982 the Z440LTD was offered with belt final drive.

A smaller sports twin was introduced for 1983 as the GPZ305.

Destined for a long model run, the shaft-drive GT550 first appeared in 1983.

The Z1000R of 1983, similar to the earlier Z1-R.

Smallest of the fours was this Z400F model of 1984, an update of the sports theme.

The Z550F was also launched in 1984, again an update.

The Z750L was the update of the larger four.

Enlarged from the year before was this Z1100R of 1984.

WATER-COOLING

More important for Kawasaki in 1984 was the advent of two new models which introduced the concept of water-cooled engines having four valves per cylinder. First was the GPZ900R, a sports model that set new standards, being faster, lighter and all new, its four-cylinder engine much narrower than the first Z1 and including a balance shaft to kill the vibration level. Totally different was the KLR600, a trail model having enduro styling and driven by a single cylinder engine, but still with four valves and water cooling.

Both new themes expanded for 1985 when the GPZ600R, GPZ750R and KLR250 joined the Kawasaki ranks along with the Z400F-II, a development of the continuing Z400F, and the LTD450, a new custom model. While this kept to the expected style of raked forks, teardrop tank and stepped seat, the engine was all new and essentially half the GPZ900R unit. Thus, it had twin camshafts, eight valves, water cooling and a balance shaft. Belt final drive was fitted.

The custom range was extended further in 1986 by a radically different model that still shared the same style. This was the VN750, a V-twin in the US-mould but having water-cooling and 4-valve heads with twin spark plugs. Shaft drive was used in this case, as it was by the 1000GTR, a touring model decked out with fairing and panniers but fitted with the 16-valve, water-cooled engine under the panels. It was joined by a super sports equivalent, the GPZ1000RX, in the same form as the 900 but offering more performance.

First of a new, water-cooled, four-valve engine series was the GPZ900R of 1984, it setting new standards of performance.

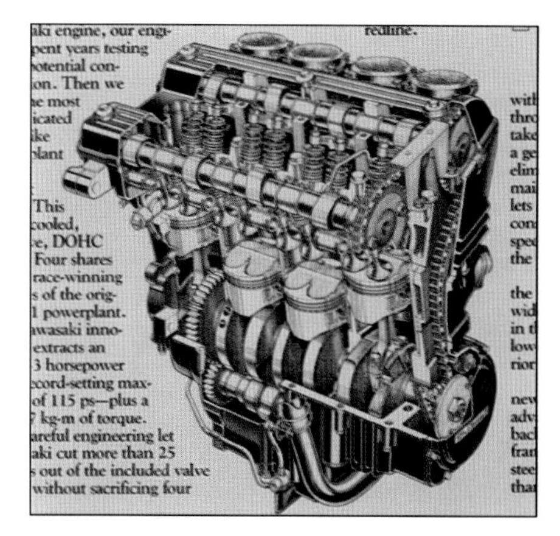

Above: Drawing of the GPZ900R engine unit showing its very compact layout.

Left: First of a new trail series, the large, four-stroke, four-valve single KLR600 of 1984.

Below: Kawasaki fours had been sprinted from the day they first appeared, but Henk Vink used two in his 1980 drag racer .

Continuing the new theme, the GPZ600R came for 1985, this being the 1990 version.

Also new in 1985 was the GPZ750R, again based on the larger four.

A smaller trail machine for 1985 was the KLR250 single, this one showing the 1990 colours.

Uprated from an existlng machine, the Z400F-II appeared for 1985.

New in 1985 was this LTD450, its engine essentially half a GPZ900R unit.

The 1986 custom range extended to a new format for Kawasaki, a V-twin engine, the VN750 in US sty]e.

Close up of the engine of the VN750, an attempt to combine Japanese technology with the American format.

Below: For the touring rider 1986 brought the 1000GTR which came ful]y equipped for its intended role.

Above: The super-sports version of the tourer was the GPZ1000RX complete with fairings.

The GPZ1000RX had a perimeter frame to house its powerful engine, seen here from above.

HYPER SPORTS

Hyper sports was the next term and, as the firm seen for performance, Kawasaki were there in 1987 when the GPX750R was added to the list, offering more power, trick suspension, less weight and a fairing. The weight saving over the GPZ750R was no less than 33kg, a substantial reduction. Alongside it came the GPZ500S, half the 1000 model in the super sports style, so light and narrow thanks to the twin-cylinder, eight-valve engine, but fast and agile in its stiff frame.

On the trail the big single was joined by the larger KLR650 having more capacity and Paris-Dakar styling while retaining the water cooling and four valves. The custom line extended to add the ZL1000 which offered laid back style propelled by a water-cooled, 16-valve engine, typical of the marque, the model having shaft drive.

Kawasaki kept up the pressure to stay in the forefront of the performance market with two more super sports models for 1988, the GPX250R and GPX600R, plus a new generation, the ZX-10. The first two followed form, having water-cooled, 4-valve engines of two and four cylinders, but the third broke new ground by fitting the engine into an all-aluminium perimeter frame to offer a stiffer structure at less weight. It was another step forward.

Meanwhile, the custom end of the range went even further with the VN15, a model in US style powered by a massive V-twin engine of no less than 1470cc capacity. It retained the twin overhead camshafts and four-valve heads, had but four speeds in the gearbox, used shaft final drive, and produced its power at a mere 4,500 rpm.

Also super-sports and a 1987 listing was this GPX750R which had power and much less weight than its predecessor.

Again making a twin from a four, the GPZ500S came for 1987 with an eight-valve, water-cooled engine.

The big trail single became the KLR650 for 1987, offering the same but more.

A big custom four for 1987 was the ZL1000 which kept shaft drive and was tuned for mid-range torque.

Small, hot twin for 1988 was the GPX250R which used the four-valve cylinder head configuration.

Larger, but in the same theme and series was the four-cylinder GPX600R.

An all-alloy perimeter frame moved the ZX-10 of 1988 into a new league.

Bigger, much bigger, was the VN15 of 1988, it having a 1470cc engine capacity so only needed a four-speed gearbox.

MORE PERFORMANCE

For 1989 Kawasaki listed two new models that were aimed at production racing while remaining fully street legal. For the superbike class there was the ZXR750, having more power and the alloy, perimeter frame, plus a racing-type fairing, trick suspension and four-pot front brakes. Completely fresh was the KR-1, a twin-cylinder, two-stroke of 250cc having water-cooling, reed and power valves, side-loading gearbox, aluminium frame, fairing, but little weight. A balance shaft went in the engine to reduce the effects of vibration and the result was a fast motorcycle. Third new model that year was the Tengai, based on the KLR650, but having a frame-mounted fairing, engine fairing and a massive fuel tank to suit its role as a green-lane tourer.

The 250 twin two-stroke became the KR-1S for 1990 when the hyper-sports range took the aluminium perimeter frame further and onto more models for the new decade. Largest was the ZZ-R1100, based on the ZX-10, next came the ZZ-R600, another four, and finally there was the ZZ-R250, an eight-valve twin. All were the pointers to the future. Alongside them was another custom job, the EN500 which had a water-cooled, twin-cylinder engine and took over from the LTD450 while retaining the belt final drive.

The high performance and large trail models usually took the front rank of publicity, but Kawasaki never forgot the need for basic machines to attract new riders, keep established ones, and offer a ladder of choice for all enthusiasts whether they sought sports performance, touring comfort, custom style, trail dual purpose, learner needs, or simply for general riding.

To this end the smaller models, and some larger, ran on for year after year. The AR series in 50, 80 and 125cc sizes, the KH100 and 125, the KE100, the KDX125, the KMX125 and 200, all had long histories and were still listed. There was a string of motocross models ranging from 60cc Juniors right through to a full blown 500. Trail models having two- or four-stroke engines, enduro models, anything to suit anybody. There were the models built for the home, Japanese, market, often of very high performance and later to reach other markets, but not always. And Kawasaki also built all-terrain three-wheelers, quads, generators and other poweres equipment.

Aimed at production racing while remaining street legal, this was the ZXR750 for 1989.

Far removed from the early Samurai, the 250cc KR-1 of 1989 had all the modern two-stroke features and was intended for production racing.

Tengai is Japanese for a far away land over a distant horizon and this is what this version of the KLR650 was meant for.

For 1990 the two-stroke twin became the KR-1S.

A new user of the perimeter frame, was the hyper-sports Z Z-R1100 of 1990.

Similar but smaller was the ZZ-R600, also a four.

Smallest of the new series was the ZZ-R250 which used the twin-cylinder, eight-valve engine.

Opposite: The new custom model for 1990 was the EN500 twin which kept the belt final drive.

Left: The 1990 AR50, smallest model of the range but with the marque style.

Below: AR80 from 1990, very similar to the 50cc model.

Quick or restricted, the AR125 featured all the style of the larger models in the range.

Below: More basic model was the KH100EX, still going strong.

And the slightly larger KH125.

While trail riders could have the KE100.

Above: Based on the KX moto-cross series was the KMX125 for the serious off-road rider.

For the more adventurous trail rider Kawasaki offered this KDX125SR model with more sophistication.

Above: Smallest moto-cross model was this schoolboy racer KX60, water-cooled and having advanced suspension.

Largest moto-cross machine was this KX500, serious machinery indeed.

The KLT200, one of a series of all-terrain models the firm built, great fun and able to go anywhere.

RETRO AND A FULL RANGE

While the ZZ models of 1990 had moved the performance envelope on, out on the street there was a growing reaction against the high technology and super-sports profile that had developed. It was time to look back, the classic movement was booming and the retro style came into being. Kawasaki's reaction was the Zephyr 550 and 750 models which returned to much earlier styling and used air-cooled engines, twin-shock rear suspension and looks akin to those of the early Z1. While the looks were from the past, the internals retained the modern technology, the 550 being based on a 400cc Zephyr already being sold very successfully in Japan.

On the other hand, the practice of producing a 750 race replica plus a race kit to satisfy street and racing needs had become harder. To side-step this, the firm introduced a new ZXR750 for road use along with a limited production version for racing, the ZXR750R. Both were totally state-of-the-art technically and wore the same stunning style and graphics.

In the same road mould came the ZXR400, based on a hot sports model built for the ultra-competitive Japanese market, but uprated to match the 750 technology. Different was the KLE500 which used the twin-cylinder engine from the GPZ500S to power a dual-role model for urban riding and a little off-road work. It featured a fairing and engine shield much as the trail models it was styled on.

Retro-style came in 1991 in the form of the Zephyr 550 with its air-cooled, four-cylinder engine.

Alongside the 550 Zephyr there was a 750 in the same mould.

A massive Zephyr 1100 was added for 1992, a year of stabilisation although the KDX125 was revised to a perimeter frame along with other changes. However, 1993 brought new models and the return of the GPX600R, VN750 and VN15, all of which had been dropped after 1990. Fresh was the KLX650 based on a pure enduro racer, softened for street use, but more off-road than most large-capacity trail models.

In looking at the retro scene, Kawasaki built the Estrella for public evaluation. It really returned to basics, powered by a long-stroke, 249cc single-cylinder engine. It had a single camshaft, just two valves, but did include a balance shaft. Fixtures and fitting were on traditional lines down to the tubular silencer but it did not catch on. Maybe too small, maybe the fitting of modern disc brakes, it was not able to create that vital spark.

An alternative that went into production was the EL250 which varied the custom line to lower it into a dragstrip format. The engine was the twin from the sports model but the chassis had twin shocks and single front disc to match its style. Maybe a new trend.

For 1994 there were two new models, one the ZX-9R Ninja, a sportster that blended high performance to a good riding position and a wider power band. The result was practical machine for everyday use, the name one used before in the USA. The other new machine was the KLX250, a street-legal version of the enduro racer, while the GPZ500S had an update and there were minor changes elsewhere.

Kawasaki had a habit of creating and forming trends. From the early singles, reliable if unremarkable, via the twins and then the exciting triples. They had finally reached the four and then took it on and on, developing and then moving the boundaries out with fresh concepts, feeding the custom market and then the retro one as well as the hyper sports. As they said before and said again in 1993 'Let the Good Times Roll'.

The ZXR750 of 1991 was built for use on the road, not production racing.

However, the similar ZXR750R was intended for racing and its specification reflected this in many ways.

Above: The hot 1991 ZXR400 four, built first for the competitve Japanese 400cc market.

Another trail or enduro model was this 1991 KLE500 which used the twin-cylinder engine.

Top of the retro range for 1992 was this Zephyr 1100, repeating much of the style of the past.

The GPX600R returned to the range for 1993, making a welcome come back.

Also back for 1993 was the VN750, seen here, and the VN15 monster.

New, KLX650, trail bike for 1993, a trail machine based firmly on an enduro model and more suited to off-road riding than most.

A variation of the custom lIne was the 1993 EL250 which featured a low line and the twin engine.

The Estrella, a 249cc single built in 1993 in the retro style and shown for public evaluation, but not to go into production.

Above: New for 1994 was the ZX-9R Ninja, a further step forward along the performance road.

Right: The KLX250 was another all-new model for 1994, reflecting advances in off-road technology.

Left: The jet ski was another facet of the Kawasaki image, this is a typical late model.

Below: For 1994 the GPZ500S was revisited to continue in its mid-range role.

KAWASAKI MODELS

No attempt wlll be made to list the hundreds of models built by Kawasaki since 1962. Below are the many basic model types, most of which were built for a number of years. Each year had a suffix letter or number, variations of this also indicating differing models. The pattern was complex but did enable dealers to distinguish models to the year. One further confusion arose in that the Z250 was not only built in many forms but also with one- or two-cyllnder engines.

What follows is a list of model types by engine cycle, number of cylinders and intended use.

Two-strokes

Road Singles	AR50, AR80, M10, Mll, Jl, Gl, GA, KC90, Dl, G3, G7, KC100, KH100, KHllO, Cl, B8, Bl, KC125, KH125, AR125, Fl, F2, F3
Mini	MTl, KV75, KD80, KDX80
Trail	AE50, AE80, JlTR, GlTR, GA3, MCl, KM90, G3TR, G4TR, G5, KV100, KE100, KM100, C2, F6, KS125, KE125, KMX125, FlTR, F2TR, F7, KE175, KMX200, F4, F8, Fll, KE250, F5, F9
MX	KX60, KX80, GlM, G31M, KX100, KX125, F21M, FllM, KX250, KX400, F12MX, KX450, KX500
Farm	G4TRA, KV100, KV175
Enduro	KD100, KD125, KDX125, KD175, KDX175, KDX200, F8lM, KDX250
Trial	KT250
Road Twins	Al, AlR, AlSS, KR-l, KR-lS, A7, A7R, A7SS
Road Triples	Sl, KH250, S2, S3, KH400, Hl, KH500, H2

Four-strokes

Road Singles	MBl, Z200, SG, Z250, BJ250
Custom	Z250LTD
Trail	KL250, KLX250, KLR250, KLR600, KL650, KLR650
Enduro	KLX250, KLX650
Road Twins	Z250, GPX250R, ZZ-R250, EL250, Z305, GPZ305, Z400, Z440, GPZ500S, Wl, W2, Z750
Custom	Z250LTD, Z305LTD, Z400LTD, Z440LTD, LTD450, EN500, Z750LTD, VN750, VN15
Trall	KLE500
Road Fours	Z400, ZXR400, Z500, Z550, GPZ550, GT550, ZB550, GPX600R, GPZ600R, ZZ-R600, Z650, Z750, GPZ750, GT750, 750 Turbo, GPX750R, GPZ750R, ZR750, ZXR750, ZXR750R, Zl, Z900, GPZ900R, Z1000, ZlR, l000GTR, GP1000RX, ZX10, Zll00, GPZll00, Zll00R, ZRll00, ZZ-Rll00, ZX-9R
Custom	Z550LTD, Z750LTD, Z900LTD, Zl000LTD, ZL1000
Six	Z1300